Presented by:

_____

To:

_____

Date:

_____

Occasion:

_____

Words of
Hope and Healing

"99 Words to Live By"

A series of fine gift books that offers the inspirational words of well-known spiritual figures as well as proverbs from many cultures and traditions, exploring topics that have moved and will continue to move many people's hearts. Perfect for daily reflection as well as moments of relaxation.

Words of
Hope and Healing

99 Sayings
by Henri Nouwen

edited by
Jeff Imbach

New City Press
Hyde Park, NY

Learn more about Nouwen, his writing and
the work of the Henri Nouwen Society:
Visit www.HenriNouwen.org.

Published in the United States by New City Press
202 Cardinal Rd., Hyde Park, NY 12538
©2005 Henri Nouwen Trust

Cover photo by Frank Hamilton. Used with permission.

Library of Congress Cataloging-in-Publication Data:

Nouwen, Henri J. M.
  Words of Hope and Healing: 99 sayings / by Henri Nouwen;
edited by Jeff Imbach.
      p. cm.
    ISBN 1-56548-227-1
      1. Christian life--Catholic authors. 2. Christian life--
Quotations, maxims, etc. 3. Imbach, Jeffrey D. II Title.
BX2350.3.N693 2005
242--dc22   2005004081

Printed in Canada

Few people in the twentieth century shaped the spiritual landscape so profoundly as Henri Nouwen. Born in Holland in 1932, he emigrated to North America after ordination to study and eventually to offer his gifts to the world as a writer, lecturer, friend and spiritual mentor.

Nouwen was blessed and cursed with an enormous life force. His prodigious energy provided the drive to study theology and psychology and to teach at Notre Dame, Yale and Harvard and to forge a huge literary output including over 40 books.

That life force manifested itself as the intense interest of a child awestruck by life. Henri enjoyed everything from a child's ball game to the circus. He kept up with hundreds of friends and was generous to a wide world of people. It also fuelled a powerful longing to pray and to follow God with all his heart. His life and books are full of his pastoral heart that others experience God deeply.

In the last ten years of his life, Nouwen's restless energy gave him the courage to move from the academic world to L'Arche. There, working and living in community among people with developmental disabilities, he felt most deeply at home.

Nouwen's vitality also had its costs. Scattered in many vibrant directions, his life could be chaotic. The drive for achievement and recognition and the anguished longing for intimacy and friendship ignited terrible unrest of soul that sometimes played out in needy and manipulative ways.

Henri learned that he could not transcend his wounds. Slowly he discovered that prayer, specifically practiced in the quiet receptivity of solitude, became the arena in which he faced his own anguish and discovered a deep call to compassionate solidarity with all people. The Eucharist, Rembrandt's painting of the Return of the Prodigal Son, and Adam, the disabled person he worked with, became Nouwen's great teachers. He learned to receive his true identity and hold his brokenness within the beauty of being chosen and blessed as the "Beloved of God." He discovered that he could continually return home to God. He learned in community he could become like the Father in Rembrandt's painting, who in the face of suffering offers blessing to the world.

Nouwen's big-screen life and simple, honest writing style resemble a Gospel narrative that models for us how to claim our true identity as God's Beloved amid the conflicting forces of our own egos, societal values and human injustice. Perhaps, the seeming jumble of his sayings may jolt the reader into new discoveries. Life often emerges that way. Our struggles intrude into the peace of our trust. Solitude is linked to community and prayer to peacemaking. And with Henri, we discover the surprise of God's loving presence revealed in our pain.

Jeff Imbach

The more I think about loneliness, the more I think that the wound of loneliness is like the Grand Canyon — a deep incision in the surface of our existence which has become an inexhaustible source of beauty and self-understanding. . . . The Christian way of life does not take away our loneliness; it protects and cherishes it as a precious gift.

The deep truth is that our human suffering need not be an obstacle to the joy and peace we so desire, but can become, instead, the means *to* it. The great secret of the spiritual life, the life of the Beloved Sons and Daughters of God, is that everything we live, be it gladness or sadness, joy or pain, health or illness, can all be part of the journey toward the full realization of our humanity.

Our calendars are filled with appointments, our days and weeks filled with engagements, and our years filled with plans and projects. . . . We move through life in such a distracted way that we do not even take the time and rest to wonder if any of the things we think, say or do are worth thinking, saying, or doing. . . . We simply go along with the many "musts" and "oughts" that have been handed on to us, and we live with them as if they were authentic translations of the Gospel of our Lord. . . . Our identity, our sense of self, is at stake.

When we have no project to finish, no friend to visit, no book to read, no television to watch or no record to play, and when we are left all alone by ourselves we are brought so close to the revelation of our basic human aloneness and are so afraid of experiencing an all-pervasive sense of loneliness that we will do anything to get busy again and continue the game.

For many of us prayer means nothing more than speaking with God. And since it usually seems to be quite a one-sided affair, prayer simply means talking to God. . . . And when it seems, increasingly, that I am talking into the dark, it is not so strange that I soon begin to suspect that my dialogue with God is in fact a monologue. Then I begin to ask myself: To whom am I really speaking, God or myself?

To pray means
to open your hands
before God.
It means
slowly relaxing the tension
which squeezes
your hands together
and accepting
your existence
with an increasing readiness,
not as a possession
to defend,
but as a gift
to receive.

What is most intimate is also what frightens us most. Where we are most ourselves, we are often strangers to ourselves. That is the painful part of being human. . . . The mystery of the spiritual life is that Jesus desires to meet us in the seclusion of our own heart, to make his love known to us there, to free us from our fears and to make our own deepest self known to us.

Somewhere we know that without a lonely place our lives are in danger. Somewhere we know that without silence words lose their meaning, that without listening speaking no longer heals, that without distance closeness cannot cure.

The mystery of God's presence can be touched only by a deep awareness of his absence. It is in the center of our longing for the absent God that we discover his footprints, and realize that our desire to love God is born out of the love with which he has touched us.

We are called to convert our loneliness into solitude. We are called to experience our aloneness not as a wound but as a gift — as God's gift — so that in our aloneness we might discover how deeply we are loved by God. It is precisely where we are most alone, most unique, most ourselves, that God is closest to us.

Often you will feel that nothing happens in your prayer. You say: "I am just sitting there and getting distracted. . . ." It might be only in retrospect that you discover the voice that blesses you. You thought that what happened during your time of listening was nothing more than a lot of confusion, but then you discover yourself looking forward to your quiet time and missing it when you can't have it.

The question is not
"How am I to love God?"
but
"How am I to let myself
be loved by God?"

We have fallen into the temptation of separating ministry from spirituality, service from prayer. Our demon says: "We are too busy to pray; we have too many needs to attend to, too many people to respond to, too many wounds to heal." Prayer is a luxury, something to do during a free hour, a day away from work or on retreat. Service and prayer can never be separated; they are related to each other as the yin and yang of the Japanese Circle.

The spiritual life
does not remove us
from the world
but leads us deeper into it.

Compassion
is the fruit of solitude
and the basis of all ministry.
The purification
and transformation
that take place in solitude
manifest themselves
in compassion.

It is in solitude that compassionate solidarity grows. In solitude we realize that nothing human is alien to us, that the roots of all conflict, war, injustice, hatred, jealousy, and envy are deeply anchored in our own heart. In solitude our heart of stone can be turned into a heart of flesh, a rebellious heart and a closed heart into a heart that can open itself to all suffering people in a gesture of solidarity.

Compassion
asks us to go
where it hurts,
to enter into places of pain,
to share in brokenness, fear,
confusion, and anguish.

The agenda of our world — the issues and items that fill our newspapers and newscasts — is an agenda of fear and power. . . . The things and people we think about, worry about, reflect upon, prepare ourselves for, and spend time and energy on are in large part determined by a world which seduces us into accepting its fearful questions. . . . Fearful questions never lead to love-filled answers. . . . Thus fear engenders fear. Fear never gives birth to love.

The same fear of "the enemy" that leads warmakers to war can begin to affect the peacemaker who sees the warmaker as "the enemy." Words of anger and hostility can gradually enter into the language of the peacemaker. . . . Then indeed the strategy of war and the strategy of peace have become the same, and peacemaking has lost its heart.

Hospitality means primarily the creation of a free space where the stranger can enter and become a friend instead of an enemy. Hospitality is not to change people, but to offer them space where change can take place. It is not to bring men and women over to our side, but to offer freedom not disturbed by dividing lines. Hospitality is not a subtle invitation to adopt the lifestyle of the host, but the gift of a chance for the guest to find his or her own.

The invitation to a life of prayer is the invitation to live in the midst of this world without being caught in the net of its wounds and needs. The word "prayer" stands for a radical interruption to the vicious chain of interlocking dependencies that lead to violence and war, and for an entering into an entirely new dwelling place.

Who am I? I am one who is liked, praised, admired, disliked, hated, or despised. The compulsion (to be loved) manifests itself in the lurking fear of failing and the steady urge to prevent this by gathering more of the same — more work, more money, more friends.

When we start being too impressed by the results of our work, we slowly come to the erroneous conviction that life is one large scoreboard where someone is listing the points to measure our worth. And before we are fully aware of it, we have sold our soul to the many grade-givers. We are important because someone considers us indispensable.

Prayer is a great adventure because the God with whom we enter into a new relationship is greater than we are and defies all our calculations and predictions. The movement from illusion to prayer is hard to make since it leads us from false certainties to true uncertainties, from an easy support system to a risky surrender, and from the many "safe" gods to the God whose love has no limits.

As soon as I say "God exists," my existence no longer can remain in the center, because the essence of my knowledge of God reveals my own existence as deriving its total being from his. This is the true conversion experience.

A life without a lonely place, that is, a life without a quiet center, easily becomes destructive. When we cling to the results of our actions as our only way of self-identification, then we become possessive and defensive and tend to look at our fellow human beings more as enemies to be kept at a distance than as friends with whom we share the gifts of life.

When our loneliness drives us away from ourselves into the arms of our companions in life, we are, in fact, driving ourselves into excruciating relationships, tiring friendships and suffocating embraces. . . . No friend or lover, no husband or wife, no community or commune will be able to put to rest our deepest cravings for unity and wholeness.

Solitude is the furnace of transformation. Without solitude we remain victims of our society and continue to be entangled in the illusions of the false self. . . . Solitude is the place of the great struggle and the great encounter — the struggle against the compulsions of the false self, and the encounter with the loving God who offers himself as the substance of the new self.

In solitude I get rid of my scaffolding: no friends to talk with, no telephone calls to make, no meetings to attend, no music to entertain, no books to distract, just me — naked, vulnerable, weak, sinful, deprived, broken — nothing. It is this nothingness that I have to face in my solitude. . . . The wisdom of the desert is that the confrontation with our frightening nothingness forces us to surrender ourselves totally and unconditionally to the Lord Jesus Christ.

People do not form community when they cling to each other in order to survive the storms of the world, but they do form community when together they erect a living prayer in the midst of our anxiety-ridden human family.

Solitude is essential to community life because in solitude we grow closer to each other. . . . In solitude we discover each other in a way which physical presence makes difficult if not impossible.

Prayer is the way out of the idolatry of the interpersonal. Prayer helps us to overcome the fear that is related to building our life just on the interpersonal, in the sense of "What does he or she think of me? Whom do I like? Whom do I dislike? Who rewards me? Who punishes me? Who says good things about me, and who doesn't?" As long as our sense of who we are depends upon how people respond to us, we become prisoners of the interpersonal, that interlocking of people, of clinging to each other in a search for identity, and we are no longer free people.

Prayer heals.
Not just the answer
to prayer.
When we give up
our competition with God
and offer God every part
of our heart,
holding back nothing at all,
we come to know God's love
for us and discover
how safe we are
in his embrace.

He sees
the depths of my heart:
I do not have to be afraid.

Underneath all our emphasis on successful action, many of us suffer from a deep-seated, low self-esteem. And so our actions become more an expression of fear than of inner freedom.

As we keep our eyes directed at the One who says, "Do not be afraid," we may slowly let go of our fear. We will learn to live in a world without zealously defended borders. We will be free to see the suffering of other people, free to respond not with defensiveness, but with compassion, with peace, with ourselves.

When we enter into solitude we will often hear these two voices — the voice of the world and the voice of the Lord — pulling us in two contrary directions. But if we keep returning faithfully to the place of solitude, the voice of the Lord will gradually become stronger and we will come to know and understand with mind and heart the peace we are searching for.

The voice of Jesus says, "I love you with a love that has no limits. Do not run away from me. Come back to me — not once, not twice, but always again. I so much want you to be close to me. I know all your thoughts. I hear all your words. I see all your actions. And I love you because you are beautiful, made in my own image, an expression of my most intimate love."

The voice of Jesus says, "Do not judge yourself. Do not condemn yourself. Do not reject yourself. Let my love touch the deepest, most hidden corners of your heart and reveal to you your own beauty, a beauty that you have lost sight of, but which will become visible to you again in the light of my mercy." The voice of Jesus says, "Come, come, let me wipe your tears, and let my mouth come close to your ear and say to you, 'I love you, I love you, I love you.'"

A spiritual life requires discipline because we need to learn to listen to God, who constantly speaks but whom we seldom hear. When, however, we learn to listen, our lives become obedient lives.

Why, O Lord, is it so hard for me to keep my heart directed toward you? Why does my mind wander off in so many directions, and why does my heart desire the things that lead me astray? Let me sense your presence in the midst of my turmoil. Take my tired body, my confused mind, and my restless soul into your arms and give me rest, simple quiet rest.

We must choose
to listen to God's voice,
and every choice
will open us a little more
to discover the new life
hidden in the moment,
waiting eagerly to be born.

Praying
is first and foremost
listening to Jesus,
who dwells in the very
depths of your heart.
He doesn't shout.
He doesn't thrust
himself upon you.
His voice
is an unassuming voice,
very nearly a whisper,
the voice of gentle love.

Being the Beloved
expresses the core truth
of our existence.

This is the mystery
of the Christian life:
to receive a new self,
a new identity,
which depends not
on what we can achieve,
but on what
we are willing to receive.

Though the experience of being the Beloved has never been completely absent from my life, I never claimed it as my core truth. I kept running around it in large or small circles, always looking for someone or something able to convince me of my Belovedness.

As a Christian, I am called to become bread for the world: bread that is taken, blessed, broken and given. These words have become the most important words of my life. They are the most personal as well as the most universal words. They express the most spiritual as well as the most secular truth. Through them, I have come into touch with the ways of becoming the Beloved of God.

Over the years, I have come to realize that the greatest trap in our life is not success, popularity or power, but self-rejection. . . . Self-rejection is the greatest enemy of the spiritual life because it contradicts the sacred voice that calls us the "Beloved."

There is a great and subtle temptation to suggest to myself or others where God is working and where not, when he is present and when not, but nobody, no Christian, no priest, no monk, has any "special" knowledge about God. God cannot be limited by any human concept or prediction. He is greater than our mind and perfectly free to reveal himself where and when he wants.

Do not hesitate to love and to love deeply. You might be afraid of the pain that deep love can cause. When those you love deeply reject you, leave you, or die, your heart will be broken. But that should not hold you back from loving deeply. The pain that comes from deep love makes your love ever more fruitful.

Downward mobility with Jesus goes radically against my inclinations, against the advice of the world surrounding me, and against the culture of which I am a part. In choosing to become poor at L'Arche, I still hope to gain praise for that choice. I see clearer now that choosing to become poor is choosing to make every part of my journey with Jesus. After all, it is not *my* poverty that has any value, but only God's poverty, which becomes visible through my life.

Handicapped people have little, if anything, to show to the world. They have no degrees, no reputation, no influence, no connections with influential people. They do not create much, produce much, or dream much. They have to trust that they can receive and give pure love. I have already received so many hugs and kisses from people here who have never heard of me, that are not the least impressed by me, that I have to start believing that the love they offer is freely given, to be freely received.

Handicapped people have little to lose. Without guile they show me who they are. They openly express their love as well as their fear, their gentleness as well as their anguish, their generosity as well as their selfishness. By just simply being who they are, they break through my sophisticated defenses and demand that I be as open with them as they are with me. Their handicap unveils my own. Their anguish mirrors my own. Their vulnerabilities show me my own.

We may be little, insignificant servants in the eyes of a world motivated by efficiency, control and success. But when we realize that God has chosen us from all eternity, sent us into the world as the blessed one, handed us over to suffering, can't we, then, also trust that our little lives will multiply themselves and be able to fulfill the needs of countless people?

Prayer requires that we stand in God's presence with open hands, naked and vulnerable, proclaiming to ourselves and to others that without God we can do nothing. This is difficult in a climate where the predominant counsel is, "Do your best and God will do the rest." We turn prayer into a last resort to be used only when all our own resources are depleted. Then even the Lord has become the victim of our impatience.

Being useless and silent in the presence of our God belongs to the core of all prayer. In the beginning we often hear our own unruly inner noises more loudly that God's voice. This is at times very hard to tolerate. But slowly, very slowly, we discover that the silent time makes us quiet and deepens our awareness of ourselves and God.

A spiritual discipline
sets us free to pray
or,
to say it better,
allows the Spirit of God
to pray in us.

We no longer experience events as endless causes for worry, but begin to experience them as the rich variety of ways in which God makes his presence known to us.

Prayer
without action
grows into
powerless pietism,
and action
without prayer
degenerates
into questionable
manipulation.

When I went to Saint Petersburg to see Rembrandt's *The Return of the Prodigal Son*, I had little idea of how much I would have to live what I then saw. He led me from the kneeling, disheveled young son to the standing, bent-over father, from the place of being blessed to the place of blessing. As I look at my own aging hands, I know that they have been given to me to rest upon the shoulders of all who come, and to offer the blessing that emerges from the immensity of God's love.

The greatest gift [for me] from L'Arche is the challenge of becoming the Father. Rembrandt's father is a father who is emptied out by suffering. Through the many "deaths" he suffered, he became completely free to receive and to give. His outstretched hands are not begging, demanding, warning, judging, or condemning. They are hands that only bless, giving all and expecting nothing.

In our utilitarian, pragmatic, and increasingly opportunistic society, however, there is less and less room for the weak, the unborn, the prisoners, the broken, and the dying. The crushed reed is easily discarded and the wavering flame easily quenched.

Visiting the sick, feeding the hungry, consoling the dying, or sheltering the homeless may not catch the public eye and are often perceived as irrelevant. But the peacemaker knows that true peace is a divine gift that has nothing to do with statistics or measures of success and popularity. Peace is like life itself. It manifests itself quietly and gently.

The fruit of humility
and compassion is joy.

Affirming life always brings joy. I have been amazed by the joy that radiates from the faces of those who work with the poorest of the poor. I expected depression and despair. But what I found among the most committed was joy. Some would say: "I love to be here with these poor people. Here I come to know Jesus and he has given me joy I never knew before."

As hard as it is to believe that the dry desolate desert can yield endless varieties of flowers, it is equally hard to imagine that our loneliness is hiding unknown beauty. The movement from loneliness to solitude, however, is the beginning of any spiritual life because it is the movement from the restless senses to the restful spirit, from the outward-reaching cravings to the inward-reaching search, from the fearful clinging to the fearless play.

Hope is an attitude where everything stays open before me. It is daring to stay open to whatever today will offer me, or tomorrow, two months from now or a year from now, that is hope. . . . Whenever we pray with hope, we put our lives in the hands of God. Fear and anxiety fade away and everything we are given and everything we are deprived of is nothing but a finger pointing out the direction of God's hidden promise.

From the moment we claim the truth of being the Beloved, we are faced with the call to become who we are. Becoming the Beloved is the great spiritual journey we have to make. . . . Becoming the Beloved means letting the truth of our Belovedness become enfleshed in everything we think, say or do.

For me, personally, prayer becomes more and more a way to listen to the blessing. I have read and written much about prayer, but when I go to a quiet place to pray, I realize that the real "work" of prayer is to become silent and listen to the voice that says good things about me. This might sound self-indulgent, but, in practice, it is a hard discipline. I am so afraid of being cursed, of hearing that I am no good or not good enough, that I quickly give in to the temptation to start talking and to keep talking in order to control my fears.

To be chosen does not mean that others are rejected. It is very hard to conceive of this in a competitive world such as ours. . . . To be the chosen as the Beloved of God is something radically different. Instead of excluding others, it includes others. Instead of rejecting others as less valuable, it accepts others in their own uniqueness. It is not a competitive, but a compassionate choice.

When we claim and constantly reclaim the truth of being the chosen ones, we soon discover within ourselves a deep desire to reveal to others their own chosenness. Instead of making us feel that we are better, more precious or valuable than others, our awareness of being chosen opens our eyes to the chosenness of others.

When we think about Jesus as that exceptional, unusual person who lived long ago and whose life and words continue to inspire us, we might avoid the realization that Jesus wants us to be like him. Jesus himself keeps saying in many ways that he, the Beloved Child of God, came to reveal to us that we too are God's beloved children, loved with the same unconditional divine love.

John writes to his people, "You must see what great love the Father has lavished on us by letting us be called God's children — which is what we are" (1 John 3:1). This is the great challenge of the spiritual life: to claim the identity of Jesus for ourselves and say, "We are the living Christ today!"

Christians today,
if they want to be Christians,
have to find the courage
to make the word *peace*
as important
as the word *freedom*.
There should be no doubt
in the minds of the people
who inhabit this world
that Christians
are peacemakers.

Nothing is more important in peacemaking than that it flow from a deep and undeniable experience of love. Only those who know deeply that they are loved and rejoice in that love can be true peacemakers. Why? Because the intimate knowledge of being loved sets us free to look beyond the boundaries of death and to speak and act fearlessly for peace. Prayer is the way to that experience of love.

A peacemaker prays. Prayer is the beginning and the end, the source and the fruit, the core and the content, the basis and the goal for all peace-making. I say this without apology because it allows me to go straight to the heart of the matter, which is that peace is a divine gift, a gift we receive in prayer.

The God who loves is the God who becomes vulnerable, dependent in the manger and dependent on the cross, a God who basically is saying, "Are you there for me?" God, you could say, is waiting for our answer. . . . Life gives us endless opportunities for that response.

Above all, prayer is a way of life which allows you to find a stillness in the midst of the world where you open your hands to God's promises and find hope for yourself, your neighbor, and your world. In prayer, you encounter God not only in the small voice and the soft breeze, but also in the midst of the turmoil of the world, in the distress and joy of your neighbor, and in the loneliness of your own heart.

Through the discipline of solitude we discover space for God in our innermost being. Through the discipline of community we discover a place for God in our life together. Both disciplines belong together precisely because the space within us and the space among us are the same space.

I was told that L'Arche's mission was to "live with" core members, so I embarked on my new life with all the people in the New House. Manual work, cooking, and housekeeping were alien to me. I was soon asked the question, "Henri, would you help Adam in the morning to get ready for his day?" I was aghast! I simply didn't think I could do this. At first I had to keep asking myself and others, "Why have you asked me to do this? Why did I say yes? What am I doing here? Who is this stranger who is demanding such a big chunk of my time each day?" The answer was always the same: "So you can get to know Adam."

As the weeks and months went by I grew attached to my one or two hours a day with Adam. Sometimes while working in my office or talking to people, Adam came to mind. I thought of him as a silent peaceful presence in the center of my life. The tables were turning. Adam was becoming *my* teacher, taking *me* by the hand, walking with me in my confusion through the wilderness of *my* life.

Adam has never spoken a word to me. He will never do so. But every night when I put him to bed I say "thank you" to him. How much closer can one come to the Word that became flesh and dwells among us?

Few are willing to lay down their own lives for others and make their weakness a source of creativity. Ministry means the ongoing attempt to put one's own search for God, with all the moments of pain and joy, despair and hope, at the disposal of those who want to join this search and do not know how.

We do not attempt our movement from our little lives into God's larger grace by simple resolve or lonely effort. When our needs lead us to grab desperately for a place, when our unhealed wounds determine the atmosphere around us, we become anxious. But then we let our hurt remind us of our need for healing. As we dance and walk forward, grace provides the ground on which our steps fall. Prayer puts us in touch with the God of the dance.

We are called
to grieve our losses.
It seems paradoxical,
but healing and dancing
begin with looking squarely
at what causes us pain.

Awareness of how such illusions grip us often comes through a crisis or hardship. In the face of a great pain or inescapable grief, we realize how little we control our lives, how feebly our protests change reality. Something happens to make us realize we can let go of a cherished ambition, bid farewell to a friend, or accept an ailing body.

Once you focus your eyes and ears on the precious center you start to realize that all the torrents of time and circumstance that roll over it serve only to polish it into a precious, imperishable gift. In this fleeting, temporary world Jesus comes to plant the seed of eternal life. It is the life of the divine Spirit within us.

Jesus would ask us: "Do you believe? Do you trust? Do you trust that God loves you so much that he wants to give you only life?" When I try to answer, I realize how far I have to go. Much in me says, "I want to be sure that there are certain things in place before I take the leap of faith." Every time I trust more I see how deep is my resistance.

All I want to say to you is "You are the Beloved," and all I hope is that you can hear these words as spoken to you with all the tenderness and force that love can hold. My only desire is to make these words reverberate in every corner of your being — "You are the Beloved."

The great mystery of the contemplative life is not that we see God in the world, but that God within us recognizes God in the world. God speaks to God, Spirit speaks to Spirit, heart speaks to heart. Contemplation, therefore, is a participation in this divine self-recognition. It is the divine Spirit praying in us who makes our world transparent and opens our eyes to the presence of the divine Spirit in all that surrounds us.

His divine compassion makes it possible for us to face our sinful selves, because it transforms our broken human condition from a cause of despair into a source of hope.

The first response, then, to our brokenness is to face it squarely and befriend it. Our first, most spontaneous response to pain and suffering is to avoid it, to keep it at arm's length; to ignore, circumvent or deny it.

My own experience with anguish has been that facing it, and living it through, is the way to healing.

We have to hold *our own* cup. We have to dare to say: "This is my life, the life that is given to me, and it is this life that I have to live, as well as I can. My life is unique. Nobody else will ever live it. Many people can help me to live my life, but after all is said and done, I have to make my own choices about how to live."

We have to drink our cup slowly, tasting every mouthful — all the way to the bottom! Living a complete life is drinking our cup until it is empty, trusting that God will fill it with everlasting life.

When each of us can hold firm our own cup, with its many sorrows and joys, claiming it as our unique life, then too, can we lift it up for others to see and encourage them to lift up their lives as well. Thus, as we lift up our cup in a fearless gesture, proclaiming that we will support each other in our common journey, we create community.

Prayer is, above all,
acceptance.
A person who prays
is someone standing
with their hands open
to the world.

We are only a very small part of history and have only one short life to live, but when we take the fruits of our labor in our hands and stretch our arms to God in the deep belief that God hears us and accepts our gifts, then we know that all of our life is given, given to celebrate.

You and I would dance for joy were we to know truly that we, little people, are chosen, blessed, and broken to become the bread that will multiply itself in the giving. You and I would no longer fear death, but live toward it as the culmination of our desire to make all of ourselves a gift for others. The fact that we are so far from that state of mind and heart shows only that we are mere beginners in the spiritual life and have not yet fully claimed the full truth of our call.

God loved you before you were born, and God will love you after you die. In Scripture God says, "I have loved you with an everlasting love." This is a very fundamental truth of your identity. This is who you are whether you feel it or not. You belong to God from eternity to eternity. Life is just a little opportunity for you during a few years to say, "I love you too."

With an eye focused on the poor, a heart trusting that we get what we need, and a spirit always surprised by joy, we will exercise true power and walk through this valley of darkness performing and witnessing miracles. God's power becomes ours and goes out from us wherever we go and to whomever we meet.

Sources and Permissions

(Excerpts are used by permission of the publishers. The numbers refer to the selection number in the present book, followed by the page number in the cited Nouwen work.)

Adam (Maryknoll, NY: Orbis Books, 1997), 78:41-43, 79:48

Bread For the Journey (San Francisco: Harper Collins Publishers, 1996), 71:June 1

Can You Drink the Cup? (Notre Dame, IN: Ave Maria Press, 1996), 92:28, 93:93, 94:57

Clowning in Rome (New York: Random House, 1979), 88:103

Compassion (New York: Random House, 1982), 17:4, 44:20-21, 54:104, 56:104, 58:116-117, 89:17

Creative Ministry (New York: Random House, 1971), 81:113, 114, 96:110

Cry for Mercy (New York: Random House, 1981), 40:26-27

Finding My Way Home (New York: The Crossroad Publishing Company, 2001), 80:77, 98:132, 99:49

Genesee Diary (New York: Random House, 1976), 48:116, 49:117

Gracias! (San Francisco: HarperCollins Publishers, 1983), 25:47-48

Here and Now (New York: The Crossroad Publishing Company, 1994), 41:17

Interview with Henri Nouwen (*Alive*, November/December 1994) 75:220

Letters to Marc About Jesus (San Francisco: HarperCollins Publishers, 1988), 7:68, 42:76-77

Life of the Beloved (New York: The Crossroad Publishing Company, 1997), 2:77, 11:63, 43:28, 45:28, 46:42, 47:26-27, 53:97, 67:37, 39, 68:62, 69:47, 70:52, 53, 90:75, 91:77, 97:99

Lifesigns (New York: Random House, 1986), 18:16-18

Living Reminder (San Francisco: HarperCollins Publishers, 1977), 13:12, 13

Organizations and Corporations

This title is available at special quantity discounts for bulk purchases for sales promotions, premiums, or fundraising. For information call or write:

New City Press, Marketing Dept.
202 Cardinal Rd., Hyde Park, NY 12538
Tel: 1-800-462-5980; 1-845-229-0335
Fax: 1-845-229-0351
info@newcitypress.com

Also available in the same series:

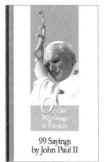

99 Sayings
by John Paul II

**On Our Pilgrimage
to Eternity**
*99 Sayings
by John Paul II*
hardcover:
1-56548-198-4, 112 pp.
softcover:
1-56548-230-1, 112 pp.

In preparation:

99 Sayings by Mother Teresa
  (Spring 2006)
99 Sayings by John XXIII

* * *

Also available:

The Golden Thread of Life
99 Sayings on Love
1-56548-182-8, 112 pp., hardcover

Blessed Are the Peacemakers
99 Sayings on Peace
1-56548-183-6, 112 pp., hardcover

Sunshine On Our Way
99 Sayings on Friendship
ISBN 1-56548-195-X, 112 pp., hardcover